The United States

Michigan

Paul Joseph
ABDO & Daughters

visit us at
www.abdopub.com

Published by Abdo & Daughters, 4940 Viking Drive, Suite 622, Edina, Minnesota 55435.
Copyright © 1998 by Abdo Consulting Group, Inc., Pentagon Tower, P.O. Box 36036,
Minneapolis, Minnesota 55435 USA. International copyrights reserved in all countries. No
part of this book may be reproduced in any form without written permission from the pub-
lisher.

Printed in the United States.

Cover and Interior Photo credits: Super Stock, Peter Arnold, Inc., Corbis-Bettmann,
WideWorld

Edited by Lori Kinstad Pupeza
Contributing editor Brooke Henderson
Special thanks to our Checkerboard Kids—Peter Rengstorf, Laura Jones, Priscilla Cáceres

All statistics taken from the 1990 census; The Rand McNally Discovery Atlas of The United
States. Other sources: Compton's Encyclopedia, 1997; *Michigan*, Heinrichs, Children's Press,
Chicago, 1989.

Library of Congress Cataloging-in-Publication Data

Joseph, Paul, 1970-
      Michigan / by Paul Joseph.
      p. cm. -- (The United States)
      Includes index.
      Summary: Surveys the people, geography, and history of the Great Lakes State.
      ISBN 1-56239-860-1
      1. Michigan--Juvenile literature. [1. Michigan.] I. Title. II. Series: United
States (series).
      F566.3.J67 1998
      977.4--dc21
                                                         97-10497
                                                             CIP
                                                             AC

Contents

Welcome to Michigan

Michigan is known as the Great Lakes State because it is surrounded by four Great Lakes. The Great Lakes are Superior, Michigan, Huron, and Erie.

Michigan has the longest shoreline of any state in the Union except for Alaska. It is the only state besides Hawaii that is divided by large bodies of water.

The two parts of the state that are divided by water have names. The northern section of Michigan is called the Upper Peninsula. The southern section is called the Lower Peninsula. Although the Lower Peninsula is only 2 1/2 times larger than the Upper Peninsula, it contains 28 times more people.

Michigan probably takes its name from **Native American** words meaning "great lake." The first people to live in Michigan were Native Americans.

In the early 1900s, Michigan started becoming world famous. Thanks to Henry Ford, the **automobile industry** in Michigan grew. People were moving to Michigan to get jobs.

The Great Lakes State is not only famous for its lakes and **factories**, but also for its beauty, people, land, and cities.

Gulls on Lake Michigan

Fast Facts

MICHIGAN

Capital
Lansing (127,321 people)

Area
56,959 square miles
(147,523 sq km)

Population
9,328,784 people
Rank: 8th

Statehood
Jan. 26, 1837
(26th state admitted)

Principal river
Muskegon River

Highest point
Mount Curwood;
1,980 feet (604 m)

Largest city
Detroit (1,027,974 people)

Motto
Si quaeris peninsulam amoenam circumspice
(If you seek a pleasant peninsula, look about you)

Song
"Michigan, My Michigan"

Famous People
George Custer, Thomas Dewey, Edna Ferber, Henry Ford, Robert Jarvik, Stevie Wonder, Gerald Ford

*S*tate Flag

*A*pple Blossom

*R*obin

*W*hite Pine

About Michigan
The Great Lakes State

Detail area

MI

Michigan's abbreviation

Upper Peninsula Borders: west (Wisconsin), north (Lake Superior), east (Lake Huron), south (Lake Michigan, Wisconsin)

Lower Peninsula Borders: west (Lake Michigan), north (Lake Michigan, Lake Huron), east (Lake Huron, Canada, Lake Erie), south (Indiana, Ohio)

Nature's Treasures

The wonderful state of Michigan has many natural treasures. Its farming **industry** is aided by the amazing soil, **ample** rainfall, and excellent climate.

The land also has rich **minerals**. Its chief mineral is iron ore. Michigan also makes and sells portland cement, sand, gravel, and crushed stone.

The beautiful forests, mostly in the Upper Peninsula, helped to make a large lumber and **wood-pulp** industry.

Michigan has around 54,000 farms. The best farming land is located in the southern half of the Lower Peninsula. The field crops consist of corn, oats, hay, beans, and wheat. Michigan ranks in the top 10 states in the **production** of sugar beets, oats, corn, and potatoes.

The Great Lakes State has beautiful lakes. The mild climate and wonderful scenery make the lakes one of Michigan's best treasures.

Michigan ranks in the top 10 states for corn production.

Beginnings

Before the arrival of **Europeans**, Michigan was a deep forest. The people that occupied the land were **Native Americans**. The land at this time was a rich hunting ground for these Natives.

The main groups of Native Americans that lived on this land were the Ojibwa, or Chippewa, the Potawatomi, the Ottawa, the Sauk, the Menominee, and the Miami.

In about 1618, Etienne Brulé became the first European to discover the area that is now called Michigan. In 1668, Father Jacques Marquette organized the first permanent European settlement in Michigan.

Michigan was owned by the French until the close of the French and Indian War. Then the English had control. At the end of the **American Revolution** in 1783, the United States finally gained control of most of Michigan.

By 1820, Michigan had more than 20,000 people. It kept growing as people from the east moved to Michigan when the Erie Canal opened in 1825.

On January 26, 1837, Michigan was admitted to the Union as the 26th state. The city of Detroit was named the capital.

An early Native American village from the 1600s.

Before 1500

The Early People and Land

Many thousands of years ago, during the Ice Age, most of Michigan was covered by huge glaciers. As it began to melt, Michigan slowly turned into an area covered by mostly forests and lakes.

The first known people to live in the area known as Michigan were **Native Americans**. They were the Ojibwa, or Chippewa, the Potawatomi, the Ottawa, the Sauk, the Menominee, and the Miami.

Michigan

Before 1500

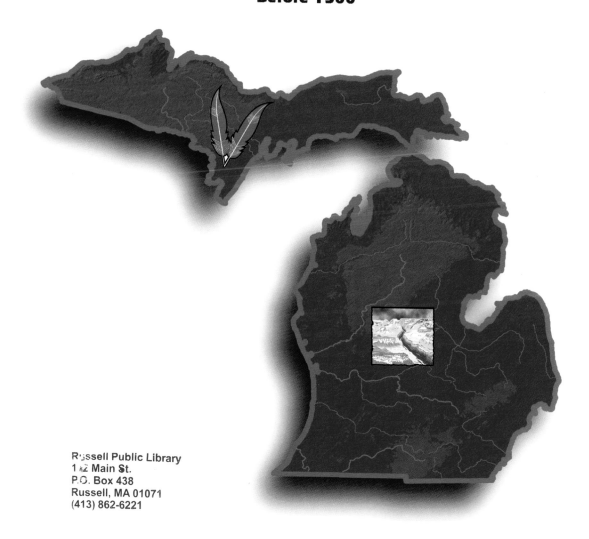

1600s and 1700s

Explorers and Settlements

 1618: Etienne Brulé, a Frenchman, is said to be the first **European** to explore Michigan.

 1668: Marquette starts the first European settlement in Michigan.

 1701: Antoine de la Mothe Cadillac establishes, or sets up, the city Fort Pont-Chartrain, which became Detroit.

 1783: England grants Michigan to the United States.

Michigan

1600s and 1700s

1837 to Now

Statehood and Beyond

 1837: Michigan becomes the 26th state, on January 26.

 1847: The capital is moved from Detroit to Lansing.

 1903: The Ford Motor Company is started in Detroit.

 1935: The Detroit Tigers win their first World Series and the Detroit Red Wings win their first NHL Championship in the 1935-36 season.

 1974: Vice President Gerald R. Ford of Michigan becomes the 38th United States president.

 1990: The Detroit Pistons win their second straight NBA title.

Michigan

1837 to Now

Michigan's People

There are roughly 9.3 million people in Michigan today. It is the eighth largest state in the country. People from many different races live there.

Many notable people have lived in Michigan. Two of the most famous Michigan residents both happened to have the same last name. One was Gerald Ford, and the other, Henry Ford.

Gerald Ford moved with his family to Grand Rapids, Michigan, when he was two years old. He went to the University of Michigan where he was a star football player. Ford then got involved in **politics**. He was elected **congressman** from Grand Rapids and served for 25 years. On August 9, 1974, he was sworn in as President of the United States. Ford was known for his honesty, hard work, and determination, but most of all, for being the only president in history to not be elected.

The other Ford was Henry. Henry Ford was born near Dearborn, Michigan. In 1903, he started Ford Motor Company. The company went on to **manufacture** millions and millions of cars. Ford made the **Model T** and **assembly line** household words. He also helped Michigan grow in size by creating thousands of jobs.

Other notables of Michigan include the amazing talent of singer-songwriter Stevie Wonder. Wonder, who was born blind in Saginaw, Michigan, has won 15 Grammy awards for his overall musical talent.

Stevie Wonder

Henry Ford

39th President Gerald Ford

Splendid Cities

Michigan's largest city is Detroit. It is the only city in the state that has more than one million people living in it. It is known as the Motor City because it is the **automobile** capital of the world. More cars are made in Detroit than any other city in the world. Detroit is a major Great Lakes Port. It also has large steel **factories**, rolling mills, and many other **industries**. Besides industry, Detroit also has a lot to offer. It is also known as Motown, because of the local record company that is in Detroit. It has produced many great artists such as the Jackson Five, the Supremes, Stevie Wonder, and one of the hottest groups today, Boyz to Men. Detroit also offers wonderful museums, the University of Detroit-Mercy, Wayne State University, and many professional sports teams.

Grand Rapids, roughly five times smaller than Detroit, is the second largest city in Michigan. It is a transportation center that is well known for **manufacturing** furniture.

Lansing is the state capital and is the fifth largest city in the state. Ann Arbor is a college town known for the University of Michigan.

Detroit Renaissance Center.

Michigan's Land

Michigan's area is 56,959 square miles (147,523 sq km) including 1,573 square miles (4,074 sq km) of water surface. During the Ice Age, thousands of years ago, Michigan was covered with huge glaciers. As it melted it divided the state into two distinct regions.

The Superior Upland covers the western half of the Upper Peninsula. This is a rough, forested region.

The highest point in the state is Mount Curwood at 1,980 feet (604 m). The Ontonagon River, which flows into Lake Superior, is the largest of the region's many streams.

The second region is the Lake Plains. This area covers the eastern half of the Upper Peninsula and the entire Lower Peninsula. In the Upper Peninsula of this region are several swampy areas.

There are many major rivers in this region. The Tahquamenon River empties into Lake Superior. The Menominee, the Escanaba, and the Manistique all flow into Lake Michigan.

In the Lower Peninsula of this region, the land has plains that are flat to gently rolling. There are farms, lakes, and many rivers.

Michigan has beautiful forests and rivers.

Michigan at Play

The people of Michigan enjoy the wonderful beauty of their state. The Great Lakes State also draws millions of visitors. **Tourists** spend around 16 billion dollars per year in the state of Michigan.

Michigan is a summer and winter playground for people. In the Upper Peninsula there are rugged mountains. People visit the mountains to ski and see beautiful scenery. Forests are filled with animals to look at or hunt. Fish swim in the rivers and streams.

In the summer months people can't get enough of the Great Lakes. People can fish, swim, and try many water sports. On the northwest coast of Lake Superior is Isle Royale, a national park. There are also many state parks along the lakes and in the forests.

Mackinac Island is a great place to visit. The island is located between Lake Michigan and Lake Huron. It has many **resorts** and hotels. You can observe the beauty by walking, biking, or riding a horse. No motor vehicles are permitted on the island, so it is very quiet and peaceful.

If people want a little more action, one of the big cities can provide that. Detroit has wonderful museums, theaters, and sporting events. Baseball's Tigers, football's Lions, basketball's Pistons, and hockey's Red Wings all play in Detroit.

Even the winters are fun in Michigan.

Michigan at Work

The people of Michigan must work to make money. Most people in Michigan work in **manufacturing**. Starting in the early 1900s, making cars was the big business in the state. Today, building cars still is big business in the state.

About 22 percent of the workers in the state of Michigan are employed in manufacturing. Michigan leads all states in the making of **automobiles**. Nearly one third of the nation's cars are produced by Michigan **assembly lines**.

Because of the many forests in the state, lumber manufacturing is a big business in Michigan.

Michigan also has 54,000 farms, making **agriculture** a big **industry** in the state. Dairy products, such as milk, along with cattle are the two biggest products. Field crops such as corn, hay, beans, and wheat are also grown in the Great Lakes State.

Because of the four Great Lakes surrounding Michigan, many people in the state work in the fishing **industry**. The fish that are caught and sold the most are, chub, whitefish, yellow perch, lake herring, yellow pike, carp, and catfish.

A fine climate, beautiful scenery, and breathtaking lakes makes **tourism** one of the biggest businesses in the state. With all of the visitors to Michigan, many people work in service jobs. Service is cooking and serving food, working in banks, hotels, and restaurants to name a few.

Because of its beauty, people, land, and lakes, the Great Lakes State is a wonderful place to visit, live, work, and play.

Manufacturing new GM cars in Detroit, Michigan.

Fun Facts

•When Michigan joined the Union, Detroit was named the capital. In 1847, the capital was moved to Lansing where it still is today.

•The highest point in Michigan is Mount Curwood. It is 1,980 feet (604 m) tall. The lowest point is Lake Erie at 572 feet (174 m).

•Michigan is the 22rd largest state. Its land takes up 56,959 square miles (147,523 sq km). The state would be the 10th largest if the Great Lakes and Lake St. Clair were land instead of water. Michigan is surrounded by more water than any other continental state.

**Opposite page:
Muskeran State Park,
Lake Michigan.**

Glossary

Agriculture: another name for farming.

American Revolution: the war that gave the United States its independence from Great Britain.

Ample: more than enough of something.

Assembly Line: an arrangement of machines and people where work passes from person to person in a direct line until the work is complete.

Automobile: (car) a four-wheeled vehicle made to take people where they need to go.

Congressman: a person elected by the people to represent them and make laws.

European: people who originally come from countries in Europe such as England, France, Germany, Italy, etc.

Factory: a building where things are made with machines.

Industry: many different types of businesses.

Manufacture: to make things by machine in a factory.

Minerals: things found in the earth, such as rock, diamonds, coal, etc.

Model T: one of the first cars made in the United States and also one of the most popular.

Native Americans: the first people who were born in and occupied North America.

Politician (politics): working as or for an elected official who makes laws for the city, county, state, or country.

Production: to produce, or make something.

Resort: a place to vacation that has fun things to do.

Tourism: an industry that serves people who are traveling for pleasure, and visiting places of interest.

Tourists: people who travel for pleasure.

Wood-pulp: wood that is ground up with water, to make paper.

Internet Sites

Virtual Michigan
http://www.virtualmichigan.com
Welcome to Virtual Michigan, the biggest list of Michigan resources. Over 100 cities and 550 unique links.

Woodstein's Universal Guide to the Motor City
http://www.bloomfield.k12mi.us/wbfh/woodstein/newsman.html
A mega-link page to Detroit and Michigan tourist spots, information sources, sports teams and entertainers.

Michigan's Internet SuperStation
http://www.ring.com/michigan.htm
Events, Sights, Travel, Zoos, Tours, Info, Shopping and more!

These sites are subject to change. To find more sites go to your favorite search engine and type Michigan.

PASS IT ON

Tell Others Something Special About Your State

To educate readers around the country, pass on interesting tips, places to see, history, and little unknown facts about the state you live in. We want to hear from you!

To get posted on ABDO & Daughters website E-mail us at "mystate@abdopub.com"

Index